THE **WARRIORS** OF **HARVEY HOUSE**

AN EXPERIMENT IN RECOVERY

Roger G.

Rincon Valley Publishing
75 Blue Jay Way
Santa Rosa, CA 95409

ISBN: 978-1-935736-05-09

Cover and book design by
Christopher C.B. Telemann
www.telemann.ink

Set in P22 Underground and Adobe Caslon Pro.

ACKNOWLEDGMENTS

First, I want to acknowledge Enrique for suggesting over forty years ago that I be the one who brings Harvey House to you. I thank the many friends who encouraged me with their love and support. Thanks to Katy Byrne and David Colin Carr, my wonderful editors, who taught me so much about the writing business, and led a novice writer through this new endeavor. Special thanks to Roger Brown, medical society executive and Buddhist priest and Claire Stuber, proof reader, both who suggested I might be a decent writer. Then there's Charlene, my life partner, the love of my life, and typist extraordinaire, who typed and retyped Harvey House a couple of times without complaining and always encouraged me. Last of all, I thank God, who kept me alive so that at age eighty-one I could still have enough brain cells left (even after drinking for twenty-six years) to write *Harvey House*.

"His craving for alcohol was the equivalent on a low level, of the spiritual thirst of our being for wholeness."
Carl Jung, in a letter to Bill W., the cofounder of Alcoholics Anonymous.

"To fall into a habit is to begin to cease to be."
Miguel de Unamuno

This book is dedicated to Bill Hopper M.D.

Bill: "Why don't you write a book?"
Me: "I've thought about it but . . . . "

INTRODUCTION

"Mi hermano" Enrique nudges me from our past: people have to know how a bunch of addicted losers turned a challenge into a winning enterprise. They need to hear about the unique talent of Eddy, whose different view of the world helped save the lives of countless veterans.

When I explained to professionals in the addiction field about Harvey House's crazy group process, they looked at me, without exception, as though I was hallucinating.

"You can't do that!" The conventional is often intolerant. The unconventional threatens the comfort of functioning in conventional ways.

And Harvey House was unconventional!

Yet there was something there – something that attracted them from the streets of skid row, from Wino Heaven, from farms and fields. The word got out and they came. The word was out that we weren't like the halfway houses – we did stuff. We had groups. We had family events for the wife and kids. The food was pretty good. You could have a picnic on the lawn. It was just for veterans.

Was it the extra effort? Or was it love?

Unless you were a snowbird, needing a warm nest,

your application for the program was a confession that you might have a passing interest in getting well. You might actually want to change your life and embark on a new path. Maybe you were just tired of living that old way, or maybe you just wanted to see what a new way looked like. If you wanted it to work for you, Harvey House worked.

With alcoholism generally, the sad fact is that very few get into recovery and stay in recovery! The National Institute on Alcoholism and Alcoholism Recovery reports that each year 35.9% go into recovery. But those numbers are self-reported. So who knows? How many Harvey House guys stayed in recovery? Don't know, and probably never will.

The thing that made Harvey House attractive, I think, is the thing that made it work. We were doing something. There was therapy happening. There was honesty happening. There was spirituality happening. There was love happening.

Once, the Psychiatric Department at the hospital sent us two veterans who had been under their outpatient care for years, and on Thorazine all that time. The psychiatrists said they drank too much. We decided to work with them, provided they were off their meds.

They were not the most active participants. They attended group faithfully, did chores, and attended all functions. They would call themselves alcoholic if pressed, but clearly they really didn't believe it. They stayed with us for a long time. Eventually we found them an apartment. Last I heard they were functioning okay.

I think the psychiatrists were testing us. They wanted to see if we could help change the lives of guys. Long term, who knows how it played out?

Harvey House helped hundreds of men. There was no way we could do an accurate statistical analysis of rates of sobriety or who returned to drinking. It was a herculean effort just to help those who were willing to show up. After they left and returned to their lives or tried to build a new life – who knows? At least they experienced sober living for a while.

~

CHAPTER I

ALCOHOL: WHY DRINK?

Why does anyone drink?

They enjoy it. It is convivial and it tastes good. Ah, but there is another reason for drinking: the feeling of euphoria. You drag your ass into a bar after a hard day's work and experience the rush, the pleasure – oh my!

"I'll have another one of those, please!"

Relief, freedom, relaxation. On top of it, damn Sam, it he'ps ya unwahnd. "I felt like crap when I walked through that door. But now I'm ready. I'll have another one of those, please!"

Then there is the frame of mind. My own first drunk: I was eleven. My friend and I took a bottle of cheap ruby port from his folks' liquor cabinet. We finished it. I was drunk belligerent and took a swing at him. He dumped me into a watering trough, where I threw up. Not what one would call an overall pleasant experience. Budding alcoholic that I was, I was already thinking about the next time and how it would have a different outcome. Next time? What the Hell you talking about next time? That was a miserable experience!

It was? It felt so good.

Alcohol: Why Drink?

Oh yes. Delusional? Selective memory? Yes and no. Just a case of alcoholism in its infancy. A human being whose thinking, understanding of, or insight into drinking alcohol is totally impaired.

"Next time it will be different."

Such optimism! Of course it will be different. This was my mantra. It was the thought that would predominate for the next 26 years, even as my life deteriorated, as I sank into a social abyss, into the lonely life of a daily drinking alcoholic: the next time will be different.

Denying always denying.

"Oh Hell, I can stop any time I want to. I just don't want to right now!"

Occasionally a bit of reality would visit and I would see that I really couldn't stop. The daily routine of waking up and having that first drink before anything else was the tip off. The shakes, the occasional hallucinations, the loss of friends – all subtle hints of what was really happening.

"I think I'll have to do this for the rest of my life. Things have really turned out poorly. Crap!"

I was not an isolated case. Actually I was pretty commonplace. Ordinary, in fact.

I theorize that I was genetically predisposed. I took to drinking like a fish to water. It was in my Mom's family. My three beautiful aunts – they started living together in their old age and drank themselves to death.

Alcohol: Why Drink?

I'd say that was evidence enough.

Wreckage is what one leaves behind when all is said and done. Ruined families, wrecked friendships, human detritus strewn behind on the road to ruin.

I don't like to talk about my own meanness and dishonesty. But I can't leave you thinking I was some kind of nice guy, because I wasn't. Angry, selfish, self-centered to the extreme, wholly without any compassion. That's the vehicle I was driving as I careened through my life.

I could be funny, I could chord my guitar and sing you a pretty song, but backed against the wall, I was nasty and uncaring. Cold, hard. Brutal, sometimes.

As I was leaving my family behind, I rented a small, unfurnished cottage in Oakland. I went back to our home and took the couch and chairs from the family room. The kids were home. I remember the frightened, confused looks as I came in and did my deed. I left without so much as a "how – do – you – do?"

That was so many years ago, but even today as I tell you about it, my heart gets heavy and my eyes tear up. Without the alcohol I'm sure I would have never done such a thing. But I did. I confessed those things in my inventory. I have made my amends. But some of that ugly stuff can still punch me in the gut.

CHAPTER 2

~

THE OPTIONS

After a period of time – maybe days, weeks, or months – addiction happens. The drug of choice is now in control. The alcohol addict has none. The element of choice is gone. A cruel, spirit-crushing routine ensues as the alcohol addict must maintain certain blood levels at all times.

The addiction has brought about profound changes in the physiology of the brain that respond in a predictable way. In the presence of the drug, intoxication or a sense of well-being is present. Euphoria is the immediate response. This is the feel-good action that is present in all drugs of abuse. If it didn't make you feel good, why use it? Feeling good has it own reward! This is the psychological process of the addicted brain!

And in the absence of the drug, nasty and painful things happen. Unhappiness, discomfort, depression, and fear take over from peace and pleasure – the opposite of the wonderful mood created by the drug. If the drug is a depressant, then physical agitation, restlessness, and severe tremors begin. If the drug is a painkiller, then generalized pain is dominant. Whatever one enjoys about the drug invokes the opposite feelings and conditions. What one seeks in the drug now reverses and bites one in the butt! Then fear of withdrawal feeds its use.

Now along comes an urge to change. Professional treatment sources are consulted. Medical intervention takes place. Pills or other medications are used to ease the withdrawal. One has stopped! But what about staying stopped?

Through the ages, alcoholism has been a thorn in the side of humanity. Imagine: for centuries there was no organized source of help for alkies. Lock 'em up and throw the key away was the answer in the 1800s. In Ireland in the early twentieth century, there was the Matt Talbot Society. The Catholic Church of Ireland endorsed a spiritual approach to abstinence. Combining strict adherence to Catholic dogma with a measure of self-punishment, some were able to maintain abstinence. A small beginning.

The neglect and ignorance of the centuries changed in the 1930s. The famous Swiss psychiatrist, Carl Jung, advised a wealthy American patient that the only hope for him was to find a spiritual answer to the dilemma of his addiction to alcohol. The patient came back to the States and through a series of events, Alcoholics Anonymous was founded.

The unscientific, mystical consultation with a "power greater than one's self" seemed to help hundreds of hopeless people. The most egotistical, selfish, self-centered people on earth began to live lives of spiritual devotion. Not religion, but spiritual principles of their own choosing. Not only that, they turned the focus of their lives to helping others.

The "spiritual" answer had been around for centuries, but it was never organized. Members of AA gave credit to a "higher power" for their sobriety. Not themselves, but a deity of their choosing. Some loving presence out there in the universe that mysteriously did what no man could do. "Of myself I am nothing," many have been heard to say.

Lives were restored. Families were healed. Careers were saved. It was pretty heady stuff in the 1930s! And all because an addicted loser chose to try to exercise faith in his or her life. It was an event that shook the world. A drunken stockbroker and a drunken proctologist started the spiritual movement of the twentieth century! Based on faith!

Who ever thought this old atheist (me) would be basing much of his life on a matter of faith? The most important element in my life is sobriety. All things spring from there. Without it, I'm not functional and my addiction is a severe, all-powerful dictator of my life. With it, I can endeavor to excel. I have never doubted that my God has a plan for me.

As I look back, the evidence of His presence in my

life shows itself. At two years of sobriety, I was inspired by the suicide of an old drinking buddy (a brilliant young internist) to design a diversion program for doctors in California. The program had been invented by a doctor in Georgia. The whole thing came to my attention by accident. Really?

As the whole thing began to come together, two recovering doctors came into my life. Really? They had the juice to take it to the places that counted! I'm sure that the Medical Association would have never listened to this polyester clad character from the National Council on Alcoholism in Los Angeles. But give them an internist and addictionologist from Orange County, and an OB-GYN from Palm Springs? Oh yeah, baby. They listened!

Then it was on to the State Licensing Board. They listened too!

The next fiscal year the Sate of California had a Diversion Program for addicted physicians!

No one knew but me. When I got word that the program had been approved, I walked outside and sat on a bench at a bus stop and talked to my late internist friend. "Okay, Jack, look what we've done. Something good just had to come out of all the ugliness. Thank you, my friend. I think we've joined the human race."

How could anyone say with conviction that all that was just coincidence? I never thought that for a moment!

CHAPTER 3

~

EARLY HISTORY

I was raised in the heyday of the lumber boom in Northern California and Southern Oregon. My father was a self-taught engineer who became sought-after as an expert on sawmills and how they work. He had gone to school in Canada but never got past the eighth grade. Yet he helped a math major friend of mine at Humboldt State College pass calculus!

The old man liked his booze. One of my early and most vivid memories of him was bringing home some of the men from whatever sawmill he was building at the time and breaking out a bottle of whiskey. All of them stood in the kitchen knocking back straight shots. Their camaraderie seemed special and manly. Those construction workers and mill hands were real men, and I wanted that when I grew up.

Sawmills were the center of our universe. When Dad took us for a Sunday drive, we didn't go see the sights. We went to look at a sawmill. I remember him sighting along his thumb at the underpinnings of some mill. "That son of a bitch isn't plumb!" Dad's mills were plumb, not listing by a fraction of an inch.

We once lived in a little town in Mendocino County

that had three mills running at the same time. In those days mills had burners – a conical sheet metal structure that had a screen on top. Sawdust and scrap lumber were fed into the burner all day long so it could be economically disposed of. On a clear, windless day little burnt pieces of sawdust filtered out of the screen and disbursed all over town. Black burnt sawdust covered everything. "Hell, it don't hurt nothin.'"

During much of my youth, I worked in sawmills. I worked in a sawmill while I was going to college in Arcata. One summer I had a job in the woods. All of those jobs are hard and dangerous. After my job in the woods, I swore I would never work that hard again in my life. I never did.

One night my best friend Johnny B. and I were drinking in a bar on Two Street in Eureka. We were more than a little hammered when three Native American guys walked in. Brandy had a few words with one of them. Big mistake. Brandy and I were in pretty good shape from working in the sawmills, but our opponents were crafty and adept. They cleaned our clocks.

We went outside and sat on the sidewalk to recuperate when we heard sirens in the distance. We were a mess – bloody and wounded. Johnny B. was talking about going back inside and wreaking revenge. I grabbed him, got him in the car, and made our escape. Safe and free, but not very sound.

Years later in an AA meeting in San Francisco, a very large longshoreman came up to me and said, "I know you."

"You do?"

"Yeah, you used to come to that little bar on the waterfront in Eureka and play your guitar and sing for free drinks."

"Well, I'll be damned!" I said. Not sure it felt good to be remembered that way.

CHAPTER 4

~

TRYING SOBRIETY
ON FOR SIZE

My life was at a standstill. My singular focus was driven totally by the physical and mental compulsion to drink. From the moment I got up until bedtime, I had to feed the voraciousness devouring my psyche and my character. In my enslavement I saw no way out. I don't know what kept me going. I was convinced I would have to live that way for the rest of my life.

There's no way I could have predicted what sobriety would bring.

I was on my way to Arcata, a familiar place, with some people I knew. A good place to begin my new life in the lower 48. Juneau was behind me. I had gone up there because Camille wanted to. We had met in Oakland and became a couple. She was a cleaned up junky, but for some reason tolerated my drinking. Our common interest was music. We got a gig at The Red Dog Saloon playing our Martin guitars and singing folk songs for seventy-five bucks a night each and all we could drink.

Then Camille kicked me out. I was on my own. I got a job on a boat that guided clients into the wild to hunt Grizzlies. I was barely able to maintain sanity on that boat because of the "no drinking before the hunt" rule the skipper had laid down. It was pure torture to wait for that first drink. But it gave me money to get back home.

In Arcata I got a room at the old, run down hotel on a corner of the plaza. And a job as a part time bartender at the sleaziest bar in town. I had arrived!

One night a very pretty, sexy lady came into my bar. She had brown hair, green eyes, creamy skin, and a killer figure. Oh my! I was smitten. Velma was running away from a bad marriage. God knows why, but she found me attractive. Oh yes, she had five kids.

We got married and moved to the Bay Area. I got a job as a salesman at a dental supply house – good salary, company car, expense account. Calling on dentists, selling them supplies. Convinced everything would be okay. But my alcoholism didn't go away. And I was supplementing booze with reds (seconal), in the fashion of the time.

I would wake up with the shakes, maybe some minor hallucinations. The immediate remedy: drink and use some more. That calmed me right down so I seemed to function in a normal way. I did smell a little boozy though.

So there we were, renting a nice tract home, the kids in school, and me with a bad case of late stage alcoholism, which I assumed I was hiding from everyone at work. What a comeback. It seemed I would be okay after all. Maybe I wasn't an alcoholic – just a heavy drinker.

Until Velma got tired of it. I think it scared her. After all, what was going to happen to her and the kids? She began to give me "it's me or the bottle" ultimatums. With my most sincere assurances, I convinced her she was the clear choice.

Now I had to hide it. The flush tank of the toilet was good for hiding bottles. My reds were taped under furniture. We could still smoke weed together because she liked it. Ah yes, cannabis-induced bliss. The American dream couple.

I got fired. Something about non-production. Leaving me without a car. I bought an old Pontiac Tempest and we moved into a cramped apartment. I had to economize with cheap wine. The ultimatums came more rapidly and threatening so I'd run off to Arcata to hide out for a few days. Then we would make up. I would make promises, all would be well. I was grateful to be back in the warm bed with dope taped under the furniture.

One more ultimatum, one more drive to Arcata. Meanwhile I'd discovered the mixed drinks in little aluminum cans. Easy to hide the empties under the front seat. And easy to drink while driving.

I took a short cut from the East Bay to Sonoma County on a back highway that ended in Petaluma. On the way, there was a new stop sign that hadn't been in place before. The car in front of me stopped for a newly placed stop sign. I nicked his right rear fender with my left front. Nothing really serious, but the car was a new Ford Fairlane 500, top of the line. The driver was not happy. I pulled into the front of the old service station on the corner and waited, with my windows rolled up and my engine running. The other driver spent a few minutes yelling then retreated back to his car. As I sat there, I pondered making an escape. I had no license (long expired) and no insurance.

The Highway Patrolman appeared. I watched as he listened to the other driver. He was getting an earful. I thought, "Oh boy".

He came to me and asked if I'd been drinking. (How did he guess?) Any alcoholic will tell you the standard response: "Sure, I had a couple of beers." The officer wrote me up for an expired license. And sent me on my way. Don't ask me why, I don't know. It wouldn't have happened in this day and age, that's for sure.

I stopped in Santa Rosa to restock my supply of canned drinks. The next thing I remember was trying to get off the freeway in Ukiah. I managed to drive off the exit ramp and end up down the embankment. I left the car and began to walk along the freeway to find a phone. I needed a tow truck. As I was strolling along the highway, a Mendocino County Sheriff pulled up. He wisely decided that I should spend the rest of my evening in the local slammer in Ukiah. My car was taken to an impound yard.

The next day I was back on Highway 101, my canned cocktails replenished. Much of the drive was spent in a blackout – a state of memory loss caused by the alcohol. I picked up a hitchhiker, but don't remember much about him. I do remember a Highway Patrolman pulling alongside me, giving me the once over, and, much to my relief, speeding off. I woke up the next morning in Eureka, parked at a drive-in restaurant passed out on the front seat of my car with greasy French fries congealed to my cheek. Was that the point I realized the party was over?

I don't know how many days I spent in Arcata. I connected with old friends who reluctantly let me camp in their back room. Every day, while they were at work, I went to the supermarket, stole a bottle of wine, and returned to the house. I closed the curtains and drank the wine in a state of severe paranoia. I knew "they" were coming to get me. Who was "they?" No idea.

I'm not quite sure how else I occupied those days.

Velma moved back to her home in Fresno. She talked to the VA Hospital about me. They told her I was probably an alcoholic. If she could get me down there, they might be able to help me with a new program they had started for alcoholism. She called all the bars in Arcata and found how to get in touch with me. I agreed to find a way to get to Fresno.

I don't know how I got the money. I had sold my car for drinking money and my wallet was empty. Somehow I acquired enough for a one-way Greyhound ticket to Fresno. Armed with a quart of Martinis and everything else that mattered in a Safeway shopping bag, I settled in for the twelve hour journey.

Velma was there to meet me. No, she wasn't going to take me home. She took me straight to the hospital. A doctor examined me in the emergency room. After feeling my liver he told me I had about six months to live if I continued to drink. *What a liar*, I thought. They escorted me upstairs to meet a skinny little man who looked like an egret with a pair of glasses and a tie. He said he was a sober alkie and that I could be too. Clearly, he didn't understand. I was not an alcoholic – though maybe I needed a little psychiatric help. He laughed. *What a jerk*, I thought.

I was referred to a residential facility, which in the pre-Reagan era was called a half-way house. I was there until there was an opening in the VA treatment program. I sat on the couch for three days, hallucinating and shaking uncontrollably, tormented by little creatures with sharp teeth that attacked my feet and ankles and made strange noises.

Gosh, maybe I was an alcoholic after all.

After the DTs, they appointed me the cook, in exchange for rent and a private room. So, I began recovery. Recovery required I not drink, smoke dope, or take any relaxation pills. Large order!

There was a mom and pop store down the street that sold wine and beer. One day, all alone in the house, I was attacked by the compulsion to drink. I remembered hearing of people taking it five minutes at a time. I tried only five minutes. Another five minutes still sober. Again. And again. After several five minutes had accumulated, someone walked through the front door. I noticed the compulsion was gone. I had made an effort to stay sober. It had worked!

One of the house rules was four AA meetings a week. I assured them AA didn't work for me – I had gone to meetings in Alaska but I drank again. They assured me that if I didn't go to four meetings a week, they would throw me out on the street. Meetings it was!

CHAPTER 5

~

HALFWAY, OR AT LEAST A BEGINNING

I began what seemed like drudgery – meetings, cooking for twenty men, and staying clean and sober. In Alaska I had sat in the back of the meeting, lost in my own thoughts. In Fresno I started paying attention to what was being said. I realized the seriousness of my situation.

I allowed myself to entertain the idea of God. I would sit on my bunk and ask Him if he was out there somewhere – to please show me. This was a huge and shocking change for me.

I was homeless and unemployable but I was full of intellectual arrogance. I felt superior, assuring them that I was a cool guy from the Bay Area, and Fresno was the hemorrhoid of the San Joaquin Valley. There are no bounds to the alcoholic ego. I had a big problem.

There was an old woman with frizzy hair nodding her head and grinning. She'd pat me on the back and say, "Keep coming back, Honey!"

At one meeting I was told to get an AA sponsor – someone who helps you work the 12 steps and guides you in your sober life. I asked a man named Dean who had been sober for five years. That seemed to me like an eternity.

He was articulate with a great command of the language, and spoke with a deep resounding voice. He had been a Baptist preacher. He drank his way out of that to become a used car salesman. He wore flashy clothing – lots of polyester with white shoes and belt. Aware of my atheism, he treated it with respect. But, he didn't soft pedal God for my benefit.

Over the next two years we developed a close relationship. The one thing he conveyed to me indelibly was that "the level of your anxiety is in direct proportion to your distance from God."

But I was an atheist. Oh, God!

One day I was doing some chores in the house and the phone rang. I asked another resident to take a message. He looked up from the phone and told me there was a guy who needed help. I put down my cleaning rag and went straight to the phone. The man was looking for someone to help get his girlfriend out of the clutches of a bunch of guys on skid row. We could use his car because he was too drunk to drive it.

All we had on hand was a three-wheel bike, adult size. The other guy peddled, with me standing on the basket behind him, my hands on his shoulders for balance. We peddled across Fresno to get the man's car. The two of us arrived at a place that had a bunch of customized chopper Harleys parked out front.

Oh, God this is not good! I thought.

Inside we found some bad ass looking bikers playing pool. The hostility was palpable. Long greasy hair, elaborate mustaches and beards, and Buck knives. It wasn't the Hell's Angels, but the same idea. Yet I felt no fear.

The place reeked of pot and beer. We walked slowly to where a card game was going on. I was confident we would not be harmed. In spite of the tank tops, big muscles, and tattoos. I felt calm and unafraid.

The woman was passed out on a dirty cot in the back room. Being the bigger of the two of us by a couple of inches and ten pounds, I picked her up. She looked bad.

We drove to the nearest emergency room. We found out later she had a broken jaw, a broken collarbone, and someone had been using her tummy for an ashtray! I looked at the whole situation and couldn't figure out why I had been so calm. It wasn't like me.

Some while later, I found myself regurgitating that whole incident at a 12-step education group with the Catholic Chaplain at the VA. The room was strangely quiet when I finished. The chaplain spoke. "Roger, you've been seeking something all your life and I think you found it that day. You're either too sick or too arrogant to understand what you have been given."

In that moment I was transported. My depression and anger left me temporarily. I believed there was a

Power in the universe. A Power that worked in my life. For the first time in many years, I was peaceful. Most important, I knew this Higher Power would be a part of my life. It has.

My gut tells me the experience saved my life. That realization of a Power in the universe that operates in my life. Wow!

Did I gain enlightenment or *satori*, as the Buddhists say? Was I saved, as the Christians say? I didn't have a clue. I was told to not think too much – stinkin' thinkin' had been my way. "Stop listening to your crazy head." Dean instructed and repeated.

Eventually my turn came to go into the treatment program at the hospital's psychiatric ward.

CHAPTER 6

~

GETTING IT

At 7:00 a.m. every day, Harvey House had a reading from a book for recovering addicts that had a message for each day of the year. The reading would be followed by several minutes of silent meditation – whatever that meant to each man – followed by a discussion of what the reading meant to whomever wanted to speak.

The former atheist was participating in discussions about God, prayer, meditation, and spiritual discipline.

We were seeking serenity, peace of mind. If you query any group of alcoholics about what they are seeking, I think you'll find that almost all will admit they are seeking peace of mind – respite from that busy activity going on in their heads. I heard one person call it "roof chatter," and another called it "the committee."

I recently talked to a friend who is a Buddhist priest. Many years back, he sat down and listened carefully to what was going on in his head. His conclusion: it was mostly lies. Meditation, the act of quieting the mind, has been helpful to him. As a Buddhist teacher, Alan Watts said, "If you're spending a lot of time thinking, you're spending a lot of time out of touch with reality".

Getting It

I have learned that faith and fear are opposite ends of a continuum. The point is that if you have a lot of fear, faith is diminished. Throughout life, faith and fear move back and forth on the continuum, a constant seesaw as time and circumstances challenge the status quo. Life creates the problems. Prayer and meditation are the solutions.

As my Fresno sponsor Dean told me, "Serenity is the absence of fear."

"Oh I'll be damned," I responded, not really understanding what he was trying to tell me. I was too early on the path that had begun with my rejection of atheism. The disbelief took up a lot of room. That empty space needed to be filled. It has taken many years to fill the space with faith and my new beliefs.

I realize now that this story really isn't about Harvey House – it's about what changed in me. It's about the Roger who rode out on a new horse into a different world. God had a lot for me to do. Now he's telling me to tell you.

CHAPTER 7

~

WHO WAS EDDY?

When I was first in the halfway house awaiting my hospital stay, there was a man with a blanket over his shoulders pacing back and forth in front of the fireplace muttering to himself. A man in his own private agony. That was my first awareness of Eddy. Even though he never told me what he was agonizing about, I think it may have had something to do with his wife and family and his behavior when he was drinking. He did so many awful things that he never would have done had he been sober. Like so many of his alcoholic fellows, that really haunted him.

Eddy was born and raised in Arkansas. I think his family lived back in the hills. I also think they were probably poor. Arkansas is part of the Bible Belt. Evangelical churches were common and well attended. The culture was deeply infused with a powerful and basic Christianity which deeply influenced their lives. At some point in his young life Eddy was taken with the message and became a child preacher. He would get before the altar on Sunday mornings and preach the Gospel. I expect that people saw a child with those abilities as a miracle of God. And he probably was. He no doubt attracted many worshippers.

I expect his parents were both puzzled and proud to have a son who had been chosen by God to carry His message. They must have felt that way because he was allowed to continue.

Was it a manifestation of Eddy's genius? I don't know.

He looked at life in a unique way. He had to have because the things he did and the ideas he had were totally different. Where did he get the idea of our group process? The "How ya gonna bleed?" concept was clearly original and untested. It was powerful, simple. And inspired! It was also absorbing. The men found it attractive. They would really get into it.

Eddy had great knowledge of the workings of the alcoholic mind. Occasionally he would pick up a passing remark dropped by a resident and accurately interpret it as a warning of a relapse coming. I was in awe of his knowledge and his laser-like sensitivity.

He couldn't seem to drop his "teacher" stance and just be another deeply flawed recovering person, so it was difficult to be his friend. He always wanted to "fix" something about you. His receiver was always evaluating what you were sending and he was constantly putting us (his friends) under his therapy.

But there was another side. One night Eddy and I were having dinner at a restaurant that had a bar. The cocktail waitress sensed correctly that we were a couple of drinkers. She kept coming back to our table offering to get us drinks. She came to our table one last time and Eddy said, "Lady, I don't think you really want us to start drinking in your place." He had been in the habit of writing funny checks when he was drinking. I was a troublemaker, prone to violence and creating nasty disturbances while drinking. She never returned to our table.

That was Eddy: complex, unpredictable, creative, brilliant, and I think deep inside, troubled by the moral dilemmas alcohol had left with him.

He taught me about love. He taught me how my own mind was out to get me. He kept me coming back to Harvey House long after I had started my new life, and he would come down to visit me in Los Angeles. I think he was coming to make sure I was okay. He loved me. I have a picture of Eddy and me on one of his visits. He is standing straight and tall, smiling at the camera. I am in my polyester, looking hip, slick, and cool.

CHAPTER 8

~

THE FOLKS WHO CAME

The San Joaquin Valley, like every other part of California, is a melting pot. There are the Portuguese who have the big dairy farms. There are the Armenians who have small businesses in town. There are the Italians who grow grapes, start businesses, and farm other crops.

Of course we can't ignore the Mexicans. They are always there to tend the crops and to harvest them when ready. No matter how they got here, they can be counted on to move agriculture forward. Often living in squalid conditions and working long hours for little pay, it seems that it must be worth it to them. They are always there when needed.

Then there are the Southerners. Americans from the south came to the San Joaquin Valley in two large migrations. The first was in the thirties during the dust bowl, best depicted in John Steinbeck's *The Grapes of Wrath*. The second great migration was during World War II. They were attracted by easy well-paying jobs in the defense industries of California.

Velma's family came from Arkansas and first moved to Richmond in the Bay Area to work in the wartime shipyards. Then they moved to the valley to partake in the jobs there. They lived in Hanford. They were still poor, but better than in Arkansas where things were so bad that for dinner they would eat potatoes and gravy made from bacon fat and flour.

A typical dinner at her Grandmother's house was fried chicken, mashed potatoes, chicken gravy, and green beans cooked with chopped bacon or collard greens with diced ham. That's what I like about the south. They were the "Okies," even though they came not only from Oklahoma, but also from Arkansas, Texas, and Louisiana. They all spoke with a distinguishable twang and used expressions like "y'all," and many were (like Minnie Pearl on the Grand Ole Opry) "right proud" to be there.

Their culture was imported and sometimes recreated right here in California. The San Joaquin Valley became a hub for a brand of country music that sometimes equaled Nashville. Any little bar in any little valley town that could accommodate a three-piece band with a singer became the center of the community on Saturday nights. They often wore mother of pearl snap button satin shirts with elaborate embroidered flowers and cowboys and horses. A fiddle, a guitar, and a bass or a piano could make a band, as long as they had a singer who could use the proper inflection.

In the forties and the fifties, it was The Maddox Brothers and Rose. They played all over the San Joaquin

Valley for many years. In the seventies and eighties, we heard Buck Owens and Merle Haggard. The latest is Dwight Yoakam and his premier song, "The Streets of Bakersfield."

The majority of residents in Harvey House came from that culture.

For the current generation, it's a matter of pride to have the nicest lizard skin cowboy boots and a fancy belt buckle. The accent may be gone, but the culture lingers. Patriotism was a given among these people. That's why many of our veterans came from those families. It was common for them to be called by two names by their families. Names like Billy Wayne, Verna Mae, and Audrey Fay were frequent. Most of the genealogy of these families was German, Scottish, Irish, and English – some Northern European nationalities that commonly pass on an alcoholism gene. We never saw a lot of Portuguese or Italians at Harvey House, but Northern European names were prevalent, along with a smattering of Mexicans.

That's who showed up at our door.

CHAPTER 9

~

PLAYING HOUSE

One of the men in the program offered a house stripped of furniture by an angry wife who left for parts unknown. Eddy and I visited the place. It was a nice house. No furniture, but a nice house. Eddy came up with an idea for beds at least. Steal 'em! What a stroke of genius. But steal 'em from where? The va Hospital basement, of course. Eddy knew there were a lot of old beds stored in the basement of the hospital. We could just drive up at night and take them. A very alcoholic solution.

We had an ancient '47 Ford pickup donated by a guy still in the hospital. Midnight came and the Harvey House Furniture Supply Project commenced. There were head and footboards, springs, mattresses, and pillows. Even blankets and sheets. The beds were heavy, made of steel. It was hard work. We couldn't load them all at once. We had to make several trips. In the end, we commandeered eight beds.

Establishing a household was more complicated. Cookware, chairs, tables, couches, and on and on. Eddy asserted, "No damned TV's. I don't want these winos sitting around getting slack jaws watching the damned boob tube." We went to the AA clubhouse and asked for contributions. We went to meetings around town, to the Salvation Army, to churches, and everywhere we could think of. Soon we had a serviceable house. We even had seed money – $34.88 in stolen food stamps that one of the heroin addicts in the program had generously procured for us!

Dr. Epstein, the psychologist who was given the job of starting and maintaining the treatment program, came by to look. He didn't trust alcoholics to get much of anything right. He was impressed. He didn't seem to pay attention to the commandeered beds. He agreed to refer six winos to us. We were on our way! But first, he sat down with us and talked about group process. Eddy had some unique ideas, which were part of what made Harvey House different. Dr. Epstein agreed!

Eddy announced he wanted to have some house rules posted on the wall. He typed up the 12 steps and posted them. Eddy was in charge, and I was second "in command." We thought we were starting a halfway house. Little did we know where this was headed.

We didn't stay in that nice house for long. Eddy had talked to a lawyer and found out about houses in town that were condemned for a freeway right of way. We could rent one for a pittance. The first house was on Harvey Street. Thus the name: Harvey House. It was a sprawling old two story Victorian farmhouse that had been swallowed into the city. We could increase our capacity to 15 or 20 beds.

CHAPTER 10

~

THEY WERE FOUND

The way we received potential residents was that when an alcoholic or drug addict showed up at the hospital for detox, they were referred to us. We provided social model detox. Social model detox is a method of detoxification that uses no medication. Instead, in our quiet gentle atmosphere, the TLC (our name for someone in detox) was watched around the clock, talked to, and encouraged. It was very powerful. I expect it is rarely used any more.

Great care was used in creating our special TLC room. Eddy knew what he wanted it to look like. Harvey House interior design (that's a joke) was quite Spartan – folding chairs, rundown couches, easy chairs, and shabby lighting fixtures. All clean and usable though.

The detox room was different. It had pretty curtains, subdued lighting, three beds with pretty comforters, a radio playing soft elevator music, and bowls of fresh fruit placed at the bedside. We set up a watch list so that a resident would be at the TLC's side around the clock. If the TLC woke up during the night, his watcher would reassure him he was okay and in a safe place.

A TLC was treated as a most honored guest. When

escorted to a meal, he was seated and served first. Before the prayer at the meal, everyone said hello to him and told him he was welcome – that we were all glad he was in TLC. If he had the shakes really bad, his watcher fed him.

If the TLC began to lapse into DTs we gave him the "potion." Eddy had invented or heard about a home remedy for kicking alcohol. It was disgusting, and made some throw up. But it worked – a combination of honey and vinegar in warm water. It diminished the shakes, and forestalled hallucinations.

While the prospective member was in detox, we would ask him if he wanted to get sober and go to the hospital treatment program. If he showed a desire to get sober, he had to ask the residents at the morning business meeting if they would allow him to be part of the group. The residents questioned him and tried to determine his motivation. They cautioned him that Harvey House was a serious place and that the group didn't put up with a bunch of phony nonsense.

What was the character of members of Harvey House? I have used the word "wino" not as a demeaning word, but rather as an accurate description of a deteriorated life. Street people may be another way to describe them – they were usually homeless, subsisting by panhandling, stealing, conning, or whatever worked to stay alive and drunk.

They Were Found

And they were all veterans – men who had honorably served their country. They were entitled to all those benefits provided by the VA. They had come home from war or peacetime service and, for whatever reason, had slid into addiction to alcohol, maybe some other drug as well. Some had families, wives, and kids. Some had long ago lost their family, even lost track of them as they slid into the oblivion of life on the streets. Hardscrabble, dirty, impaired, humiliated, angry, slippery. All those things and more.

Most had been shunned by society, thrown out of bars, restaurants, or public and private places for their antisocial behavior. Tossed out, ignored, jailed, beat up. Often they felt doomed to live that way for the rest of their lives – no hope, no future, no love, no caring, and no friendship except to partner up to obtain alcohol or drugs. In turn, this just fed that all powerful and demanding Jones that was their slave master. Ugly and humiliating. Without any choices but to drink and use.

But lest our compassion become misguided, let's not forget he will lie, cheat, steal, and use people to achieve his ends.

CHAPTER 11
~
WHOEVER THEY WERE

Harvey House TLC worked well, thanks to Eddy's genius.

To illustrate, there's the case of Charley Muldoon. Charley was a notorious wino. He had survived years of drinking cheap fortified wine, which was basically grape juice with 20% alcohol added. To call it wine was a stretch. I'm sure if one were to analyze the chemistry of that stuff, it would be full of toxins. In those days it sold for fifty cents a short dog (a pint). It was usually labeled "Ruby Port." Sweet stuff seemed to have more impact than "dry" stuff.

Charley was dirty and disheveled, with a demented gleam in his eye. He likely had wet his pants, lost something important such as his keys or pocket knife, and was accusing everyone within ear shot of stealing it. Charley was always ripe with a florid urine, wine, and cigarette smell. He often let loose with some of the most creative spurts of obscenities and perverted language known to man.

Charley's usual residence was an old run down motel called "Wino Heaven." It was owned by a guy named Joe Pirro, who had discovered how to make money from late stage alcoholics. It was ingenious, really. If they had a pension or some kind of income, they could get a room at Wino Heaven. They paid for it by signing over 100% of their income to Joe. In the motel office Joe had a little store, which sold cheap wine, canned goods, and snacks at exorbitant prices. He gave each resident a certain amount of credit at the store, based on the money he confiscated beyond the rent. Joe kept whatever was left over. The resident bought his wine and whatever food he could choke down from Joe until his credit was used up. The purchases always exceeded his monthly deposit, so Joe would run a tab. The residents were always behind.

It was a racket, but not illegal. If one of Joe's tenants got out of hand, Joe would punch him around a bit. Most of Joe's tenants, weakened by years of drinking, couldn't fight back. They took their lumps and stayed on, attracted by a steady supply of wine.

While I was in the hospital program, Charley came in for detox. It was a noisy and crazy experience. Hallucinations, severe tremors, and restraints applied with wrist and ankle cuffs. He never stopped yelling and cursing around the clock. Nobody was happy to see Charley admitted to the hospital. His medical records were two files, each several inches thick.

At the Harvey House TLC room he spent several days in relative peace, merely cussing out his watchers and complaining about the food. But he had no hallucinations – his cussing and yelling was relatively subdued. Charley was, comparatively, a pussycat at Harvey House detox.

Charley was in his fifties, but looked eighty. He was an example of how much abuse the human body can take and still continue to function. Charley didn't last long with us. The streets were calling and he had to go. He was soon to die.

I have no idea how many men went through detox at Harvey House, but I'm sure it was well into the hundreds. Our detox is now a part of history, a story from a bygone age. It was a demonstration of love practiced by men who couldn't love themselves. Out of necessity, they gave of themselves to another human being. It was a refreshingly humanizing experience, and one which, if they remained sober, would be practiced over and over by sponsor sponsee relationships in AA – a perpetual process of one man reaching down to pull another man to safety.

CHAPTER 12

~

RECRUITING

There were things that happened at Harvey House that stretched credibility.

Eddy decided to create a Recruiting Team of two guys. One had to have a car. We had to feel confident they could be trusted to go on a mission and return. Not many fit those criteria. Given that kind of freedom, the usual urge was to run away and get drunk. Sending men out on a mission was risky.

Someone called us one day about a guy who lived in an abandoned service station in Firebaugh, a farming town several miles from Fresno. They were afraid they'd find him dead someday in his service station home.

The Recruiting Team went to Firebaugh early one morning. It was important to go in the morning before the subject of a mission had had his first drink. They found Willy sleeping in one of the restrooms. They assured him that if he came with them, he could have a warm place to stay and three meals a day. Not only that, he would be able learn how not to drink. Willy was hurting bad from the cheap "wine" he had drank the day before. He thought it would be a good idea to learn how not to drink.

Recruiting

So Willy came to Harvey House, caked with the dirt of many days without a bath. The stench was overwhelming. The first chore with Willy was to get him in a shower. It took a couple of the men to wash him thoroughly. He needed some extra help because of his befuddlement. From his bald head to his flat feet, Willy was given a good scrubbing. Even though he complained about the procedure, he came out squeaky clean. First time in years.

He was dressed in a clean pair of pajamas and escorted to TLC.

He received the full treatment as a most honored guest. Because of the bizarre circumstances of how Willy had been living, everyone gave him a lot of attention – a kindness uncharacteristic for these men.

As time went on, Willy showed symptoms of "wet brain." That means he had suffered severe damage from alcohol, often drinking for days without eating. This is always a dangerous practice and has serious consequences. Willy was taken care of by a couple of other residents who helped him through each day. Every day was a new experience – he simply could not remember what had happened the day before.

Willy had been in combat in Korea, surviving the time the enemy almost pushed the UN troops down the peninsula and into the sea. It was a horrible and humiliating piece of history. He had attained the rank of sergeant and served bravely and honorably. Now he was barely functional.

Willy stayed with us for several months until we found him a spot in the California Veterans Home in Napa County. Willy spent the rest of his short life there. We even found some relatives who visited him occasionally. They remembered him when he was whole.

I sometimes think of Willy and wonder what kind of guy he was before his brain damage. He had a wife, children, grandchildren, and no doubt had friends. It makes me wonder what went wrong.

CHAPTER 13

~

WHERE YOU GO, HE GOES

While drinking, there is no more selfish and self-centered human being on earth than the alcoholic – putting their drinking before family, work, and even their health. *Anything* that threatens the drinking must go. It is heart breaking to think how those good ordinary values are tossed aside.

What do you do to keep a bunch of drunken mavericks in some kind of order? How do you address the seductive call of the streets and a return to drinking and using? Remember, addictions are diseases of relapse! Ask a recovering alcoholic about his drunkenness and he'll tell you that it's natural for him to be drunk. I said it before and I'll say it again – what alkies do is drink. Their life is lived for alcohol. All other things are secondary.

The practice of love was essential to the function of the Harvey House group. It was a kind of retraining, a way to turn the resident's head from himself to others.

For those who haven't lived it, that's hard to understand!

So, when you house a bunch of them in a place that's alcohol free, with everyone just a few days or weeks from drinking, it can be tough. Put that alongside the habitual lying, manipulation, and the ability to play-act normalcy and you have a powder keg always primed for a blow-up.

It is a seething underground of secret desires to once again experience the euphoria of oblivion. It's a world that is protected from reality and life as it is. The universe seen through a fog of induced pleasantness. "Oh, crap – let me go there once again. I don't need this sobriety BS."

But, there were rules. There was group living. Putting up with people you may not like very much. Chores, smells, noises, jerkwater personalities, likes and dislikes contrary to yours. Why would anyone want to live like this even for a little while? I would never associate with even half of those lame losers on the outside of Harvey House.

"But! Here I am. I'm going along to get along. Secretly waiting for the moment that allows me to slip out the door and get a small bottle of wine and fill the hole in my gut."

One of the important things that we discovered was that even though a resident might want to return to the old life, he saw others who *should* be in recovery. Some of the younger residents, for instance, who needed to start a new life before it was too late and they end up late stage and hopeless!

The question was: would they hang in?

Sometimes it was easy to spot a flight risk. When one of those appeared, we would call on a unique Harvey House group exercise called "marriage."

Eddy would begin. "Okay you've decided that you want Bill here to be a part of your group, but what the hell makes you think he's going to stay? Look at 'im! He can't wait to get back out there and die. I'd like to propose a marriage for old Bill."

The group is on the edge of their seats in anticipation.

"Bill, I'm proposing that we marry you to young Johnny here. Where he goes, you go. Where you go, he goes. If you decide to leave, we throw young Johnny back on the streets right behind you. Don't test us because you know we're crazy enough to do it!"

Half the group is nodding in affirmation.

"I'd like to have a show of hands. How many of you support this marriage?"

Unanimous! The whole thing has been supported by Bill's peers! He knows they'll be watching!

Bill knows he is obliged to do something noble! He will be responsible for another human being staying in recovery. Johnny is young – he deserves a chance to not go where Bill did in his alcoholism. He can start a new life and maybe amount to something.

Bill stayed.

CHAPTER 14

~

CHRISTMAS SPIRIT

It's no secret that the Christmas holidays are painful times for some people. Eddy and I discussed the coming season. Could we prevent a mass exodus from Harvey House? We must prevent a disaster among our residents. We knew there would be fits of anger, depression, and loneliness falling on their troubled souls. We believed that many of the men would go out and get drunk to soothe the pain of Christmases past – a perfectly natural solution to such ugliness. After all, that's what alcoholics do. They drink. The question was how to distract them from doing what they normally do?

The discussion went on for a while and finally Eddy said, "Let's get 'em to sing Christmas carols!"

"What the hell are you talkin' about?"

The idea of getting our guys organized, dressed up, and musically trained was ludicrous. Hair combed, shaved, teeth in (if they had them), nice shirts, and pants. It was a crazy idea.

"Yeah, we could sing at the VA Hospital. Just go from floor to floor singing carols that everybody knows. You know 'Silent Night,' 'Deck the Halls,' that kinda stuff."

"And who's gonna be the music director?" I asked.

"You are!" Eddy had a strange smile on his face. "I mean you got the musical background, doncha?"

"No! I can't read music and I can only play seven or eight chords on a guitar."

"Well, you're the guy to do it."

The others in the room were all looking at the floor and nodding in agreement. They knew it was useless to defy Eddy when he got an idea like that.

"Who's going to play piano for our rehearsals and our performances?" I asked.

"Put the word out at AA meetings that we're looking for a piano player for the Christmas season. And I'll find out if we can use the piano at the AA clubhouse for our rehearsals," said Eddy.

The day came. We had a nice lady who had volunteered to play the piano and we had arranged a rehearsal. The clubhouse was only a couple of blocks away. We marched over there, all 50 or 60 of us, carrying sheets of lyrics. We were ready.

The piano player hit the first chord. Total dissonance ensued. The lack of harmony made me want to find a hole in the ground to stick my head in. Our rendition of "Silent Night" made that beautiful melody sound as though the banshees had committed to destroy Christmas.

It went that way through the rehearsal. The piano

lady finally packed up her music. With an incredibly painful smile, she asked if we were going to continue. I told her I wasn't sure – I would discuss it with Eddy and get back to her.

We went back many more times. It was discouraging, though the guys seemed to enjoy it. I reminded them that one of these days we would be going to the hospital to sing for others.

Then, one day: a miracle! The voices blended. The melodies were recognizable. There was a beautiful sound. We had a choir!

Merry Damned Christmas, you all! I couldn't believe it. Our piano player was struck dumb. How the hell had that happened? My conclusion was that there is a power in the universe that makes such things happen.

We piled guys in our old beat up cars and drove to the VA hospital. We found decent clothes for everyone in our donated clothing locker. Guys who had teeth actually wore them. Hair slicked back with goose grease, shaved, proud, and looking good. We were going to stun the world with our brilliance. And we did.

We wandered through all seven floors. The Protestant Chaplain asked who we were, and one of the bolder men replied, "We're the World Famous Wino Choir, Chaplain."

We were invited to a church service in town. The YMCA Christmas Tree lot invited us to sing for four trees for our houses. We gave of ourselves. We wallowed in an intensely spiritual exercise. Depressed eyes gleamed with purpose and anticipation. Talk at dinner was about success and giving of our gift.

There were the normal bullshit tales about the time one sang at a nightclub. Another talked of seducing a beautiful girl with his fabulous voice. The familiar sort of alkie stories. Nobody believed it anyway, but the teller got a lot out of it.

The season came to an end. Not one guy sneaked away. Not one guy drank. There is a profound principle in sobriety: *If you want to keep it, you have to give it away.* And so it was.

CHAPTER 15

~

FUNCTIONING WELL

Chores had to be done. Floors swept and mopped, bathrooms cleaned, kitchen scrubbed and sanitized, yard cleaned and mowed – there was a lot to do around the houses.

It seemed to be a matter of pride to the men that their house and yard be neat and tidy. It was easy for these veterans to do the chores. It was what they had done in the military. Every enlisted man is involved in cleaning and tidying his living, eating, and working spaces.

The inside of the houses, though poor and much used, was always clean and neat. The floors glistened, the walls were wiped down and spotless. The kitchen stove was pristine. The refrigerators were neatly stacked with food, leftovers, and Department of Agriculture handouts.

Most everybody smoked. That's just the way it was with alcoholics. AA meetings were totally immersed in cigarette smoke. It was impossible for a non-smoker to survive in a meeting for more than five minutes. But smoking was not allowed inside Harvey House. It was done outside. The yard was strewn with old coffee cans for butts. It was a crime to throw your butt on the ground.

The upstairs area were the sleeping rooms. Beds were neatly arranged in each room. Upon arising, each man was required to make his bunk, military style. Although crowded, the sleeping area was always neat and clean. Everybody was awakened at 5:30 a.m.

The bathrooms were a problem. There had to be order and discipline. Each resident had a few minutes to perform his personal care. Brushing what teeth you had, shaving, washing your face – all performed in a strict time limit. Showers were scheduled twice a week for each resident. The shower was usually going all day long to accommodate everyone. Nobody seemed to lose track of their shower time.

Much of our fresh produce was supplied by an old hog farmer named Earl. He was sober and scoured the supermarkets every day for day-old produce, bread, and whatnot for his hogs. But first he would sort it out, and the best food was reserved for "his boys" at Harvey House. The food was clean and quite usable. We always had salads and fresh veggies for dinner, thanks to Earl.

Earl was noisy and we always knew when he was around. He had a grating voice that had a decidedly nasal tone. Earl the Pearl, as he was called, was kind, generous, and thrilled with his sobriety. He would tell anyone who would listen about his sober life.

He was always joking about his wife whom we never

saw. "Well boys, I gotta get goin' to the hogs or the ole lady'll kick my skinny ass! Don't forgit to remember ole Earl in your prayers, boys." Off he would drive in his squeaky old pickup with the trailer full of food for his hogs, singing an old Hank Williams song through his nose.

The kitchen was usually going all day. Even though the food was simple and inexpensive, it was nutritious and easy to prepare. Bread, margarine and jam, dry cereal, and oatmeal were usually served at breakfast.

Lunch was bread, cold cuts, jam and peanut butter, sliced tomatoes and lettuce to garnish the sandwiches. Usually there was Kool-Aid and coffee to drink.

Dinner was almost always hot and tasty. We tried to make dinner special. The most frequent dish was beans, ham hocks, salad, and corn bread. Most of our residents were from the south: Texas, Louisiana, and Oklahoma. That meal was like home to them. Another common meal was spaghetti and red sauce with salad. Once in a while, especially on weekends, there would be fried chicken with potatoes, gravy, and some sort of vegetable.

"Boy howdy, that was good eatin.'"

Nobody complained about the food at Harvey House!

CHAPTER 16

~

NOT WITHOUT SURPRISES

We got a call from the VA hospital. They had a veteran who had shown up at the emergency room and wanted treatment for his addiction.

We had organized a Welcoming Committee – a couple of the guys who would pile in one of the nicer cars and go to the hospital to receive the new man and transport him back to Harvey House. At that point Eddy and I would take a look, ask a few questions, and admit the new guy to the TLC room for 24-hour observation and care. The stay in the TLC room afforded us a chance to take a look and see what kind of alcoholic/addict we had on our hands.

One day the Welcoming Committee went to the hospital and brought back Danny Kaine. Danny was different than anyone we had ever admitted to Harvey House. When they brought Danny into our office for an interview our mouths dropped open in surprise.

Danny was impeccably dressed. He had on a very nice, worsted grey flannel suit, a button-down blue and white striped oxford cloth shirt, and a stylish dark blue tie with yellow and red figures on it. He was carrying a very nice leather attaché case. He was quite handsome, with a goatee and very neatly combed hair.

"What are you doing here?" we asked.

"I need help!" he answered.

"What for?"

"I got a real bad Jones."

"Oh yeah, what are you using?"

Danny started to squirm.

"Heroin."

I grabbed a flashlight and checked his eyes for pupil accommodation. His pupils were pinpoint and did not adjust to the exposure to light. Danny was high as a kite. Heavy eyelids, pinpoint pupils, slightly slurred speech – he was doing an opiate of some kind, alright. Eddy asked him to open his attaché case. There were some papers that identified him as a veteran.

"Okay, Danny, where is it?" asked Eddy.

Danny pulled at the lining of his attaché and about 10 nickel bags of heroin (five dollars each on the street) dropped out. Neatly packaged in small plastic baggies it was Danny's business for the day.

"Holy shit, you brought that stuff in here?"

"I didn't want to get rid of it! That's fifty bucks, man!"

Later, Eddy and I went to a toilet with scissors and cut each baggy open and flushed the powder and the baggy down the toilet. Since we were both addicted, we never did anything having to do with alcohol or drugs without two people to watch each other.

Not Without Surprises

It turned out that Danny had been working for a large insurance brokerage in town and, of course, had been fired for non-production and absenteeism. Every day he would leave his middle-class home and act like he was going to work at the brokerage. He had two teenage daughters and a very codependent wife. They had no idea what he was actually doing with his day. He would park in a certain neighborhood and conduct his business – suit, tie, and all. Nobody thought he was a narc because what narc would be stupid enough to wear an outfit like that and sell dope?

Danny stayed with us for the duration and went through the hospital portion of the program. Later, he went through a VA sponsored education program for addictions counseling and went to work in a treatment program.

Many years later, as he was dying from cancer, Danny called me. "Hey big guy, I still think I could kick your ass!"

"Yeah, you probably could Danny." He passed two days later.

CHAPTER 17

~

LIVE WHILE YOU CAN

We had several African Americans go through Harvey House. The one I remember best was Little John. He was a small man, about 5'5". His skin was very dark, black in fact. His voice was raspy and deep. Little John was the kind of guy that viewed the world in black and white. Things were either good or bad. People were the same.

He took to recovery like a fish to water – he was ready. He had no issue with the idea of God or Higher Power. The 12 Steps were the path. He was ready to walk that path.

He and Danny were inseparable. Danny was tall, handsome, and white. College educated and articulate. The two of them were a sight to behold. Each in his own way was making a bid for recovery.

They were constantly arguing. Good-natured and always for fun, they debated everything.

No one knew that Little John was dying. Little John didn't know he was dying. As he went through Harvey House, a nasty cancer was gnawing away at his insides, consuming him piece by piece. There was weight loss, but not enough to suggest a chronic degenerative disease. He complained about being tired and napped on his bunk during breaks.

One night Little John woke Eddy up. He was bleeding from both ends of his body. His hands were shaking and he was afraid.

"I don't wanna die, man!" he said as tears flowed down his cheeks.

Eddy took him to the hospital and called his mother. Little John's mother was always there during visiting. She always managed to bring some fantastic thing to eat. She loved Harvey House.

I called her Mrs. Little John, but she always said, "Call me Netty, Mista Roger."

He lingered for three or four days and then he passed. Mrs. Little John called to tell Eddy so he could pass the word on to everyone. It struck the house like a bomb. The place was usually noisy, but that day it was like a mausoleum.

It was decided in group that we invite Little John's mother to dinner so we could celebrate his passing with her. She was the first woman and the first relative to have dinner with us.

That night, over fried chicken, mashed potatoes, and homemade chicken gravy – his favorite meal – we celebrated Little John's life. His mother listened solemnly to everyone.

She rose. "I feel so lucky that my son got to die here.

We both love this place. He was happy here. I could see his life start to turn around. What a blessing. Thank you all! And before I leave I want to hug each one of you. What a gift you have given us!"

After that, it was back to Harvey House business. But it was a little quieter for several days.

CHAPTER 18

~

SNOWBIRD

There is a group of veterans that are well known to anyone who is affiliated with the VA. They usually live on a pension or some kind of government dole. They are most often addicted, and they go from hospital to hospital to take advantage of detox services, treatment programs, etc. They are called "Snowbirds."

They have been given that name because they tend to move west and/or south as the winter weather gets bad so that they end up in gentler places as the frigid weather smothers the Midwest and the East Coast.

Dr. Epstein showed Eddy and me a chart of a man who had been recently admitted to Harvey House TLC for detox. He had started his journey at a VA in Michigan, and been treated at a VA in Iowa for acute appendicitis. From there, he went to a VA in Kansas, received LSD treatment for his alcoholism, and continued west as the weather got worse. He went to Arizona and Los Angeles, and arrived in Fresno complaining of chronic alcoholism.

He sat in Harvey House TLC being treated as a most honored guest, and taking advantage of all that we offered. When he came up for admission to the Harvey

House Group, Eddy decided to share a little of his history so that the group would understand what we had on our hands. This guy was only there to use us as a jumping off spot to go back to Los Angeles or wherever. Since he was not officially in a VA facility, his health record would only show that he came for detox at the hospital and that he had been referred to Harvey House. He was a sure bet to sneak off in the night and head for his next VA hospital.

So Eddy proposed that he be married to one of the younger members of the group. If he decides to sneak off in the night, we would throw the younger man out behind him. That made the Snowbird responsible for the younger man staying in recovery.

The Snowbird scoffed and expressed his doubt that we would actually throw the young man out if he left.

"You don't want to test us. We don't make idle threats," said Eddy.

The Snowbird watched the members of the group nod their heads. Yes, they would absolutely throw the young man out if he decided to sneak off in the night.

"We've done it before, we'll do it again. Mister, you're stuck."

So the Snowbird stayed. For the first time the system had outfoxed him.

"We want you to know how much we love you," Eddy told him.

CHAPTER 19

~

STONE BOXES

There are those who go through their lives with a painful ugly experience locked up inside of them in an impenetrable stone box. Though the box causes its own pain and discomfort, it remains secret, never to be exposed to the light of others. It nags at them, impairing their enjoyment, causing loneliness and sadness. But you can't tell it's there by looking at them, except sometimes it shows itself as sadness in the eyes. They learn to create a facade of "normalcy," smiling, being a "nice person."

Alcohol is a great painkiller. It puts that thing back in the box and sits on it. It can't hurt as long as the euphoria or the stupidity of intoxication pervades. You feel free of it. It is known to the sufferer that as long as alcohol is present, it can't sneak up on you, it can't pick at the scab, and you are able to get by. Whoopee!

But eventually something else creeps into the picture. Addiction, dependency, the feeling you must drink. There is a new presence now – the threat of a nasty sickness, tremors, acute anxiety, a desperation that tells you to just drink and it will be better.

The addiction wrestles you to the ground in nothing

flat. You belong to the alcohol now, lock, stock, and barrel. It is your life. Drink up man! You and alcohol have a tight partnership – an affair of the heart, mind, and body. Nothin' like it.

Jim Moody came to Harvey House in the usual way. He went to the hospital emergency room and asked for help. Our greeting committee retrieved him and drove his '65 Pontiac Tempest GTO back to Harvey House. Everyone admired that immaculate car. It was Moody's pride and joy.

Jim was not a big man, but he was stocky and tough looking. He had a ready smile and an easy manner. Right away he wanted to involve himself in affairs of the house. He seemed to enjoy cooking, so we put Jim in the kitchen where he worked tirelessly and his food tasted good.

Jim would participate in groups, but he was clearly holding something back. None of the staff ever talked to a resident one-on-one. The group was the place for that. So Jim was never "taken aside" by anyone.

He went through the whole program – the hospital portion, the groups, and revealed nothing. Always friendly, always level in his mood.

But look at those eyes. There was a sadness, a hurt there.

In group: "Hey Jim, you look like you could share something with us today. Are you ready to talk to us?"

"No I'm just fine. I got nothin' to say."

"Jim, you and I know that's bullshit, you're trying to bullshit a bullshitter here. You're carrying something that's killing you, man. Let it out, free yourself."

"I'm okay."

"Anyone who believes that will believe anything."

He wiggled out of it again.

The time came that Jim had done everything we offered in the program. It was time for him to graduate and move on. We always gave graduates a silver dollar that had one side smoothed off and engraved with the Pogo quote, "I have found the enemy and he is me."

Jim received his coin in a big ceremony. Everyone told him what a nice guy he was and they were going to miss his cooking, blah, blah.

Eddy and I stood on the porch as Jim packed his gear and started the car, waved at us smiling, and drove away in a flash of chrome and the rumble of glass pack mufflers.

We shook our heads. He's going to stop somewhere, buy something to drink – will drink until the end. He left town, we never saw or heard from him again.

Stone box and all.

"Bye Jim. Bye-bye!"

CHAPTER 20

~

BLEEDING FOR LOVE

How do you discipline the undisciplined? How do you make discipline not look like discipline? Why even call it discipline? Can we call it something else? How about love? Yes, let's call it love!

Love is a part of recovery. Love is spiritual. Love is transcendent. It penetrates hearts of stone. It melts the steel of toughness acquired surviving the streets. It has to be an overt act. It has to be demonstrable. It can be, and often is, a sacrifice.

When you give blood, you take the essential life fluid from your body and package it to give it to someone who needs it. The recipient lacks the blood to maintain life. He receives yours and his life is sustained with a part of you. It's a gift. You may never meet the person who receives your gift, but you know someone is walking around with some of your life in them. You bled for them – what greater love?

Rudy had been to many VA treatment programs. He knew how to be a client. He smiled, he talked in group (about others, never about himself), and he was compliant. But his participation was minimal. He was hiding out in plain sight.

One day he sat on one of the lawn chairs under the tree and smoked some cigarettes, telling sea stories about when he was in the Navy – being a gunner's mate on a destroyer, and being at General Quarters (prepared for battle) and firing that 5 incher at some enemy boat a couple of miles away. "We sunk that Commie son of a bitch."

He spit as he said it.

Then it was discovered that Rudy hadn't done his chores. In a normal group living facility, someone would figure out a penalty of some kind. Often the penalty would be adjudicated and meted out by an individual – probably the head guy. That's a normal operating procedure.

Harvey House didn't do things that way. There had to be love involved.

Eddy decided to take it to the group. He called a "crash meeting." The word traveled through the house: "Crash! Crash! Crash!" Everyone immediately dropped whatever they were doing and headed for the meeting shed. A crash meeting is a dire emergency. The group is there to save a life.

Eddy began. "This house is run on certain principles of love. We are here to help each other. Some of us need more love than others. Nobody does anything in this house because it's nice or the right thing to do. We do these chores because we care about our fellows.

Our kind of love says, 'I may not like you, but I love you enough to help you if you need it.' If we lack love we aren't useful.

"I have heard that Rudy didn't do his chores this morning. Is that right, Rudy?"

"Yes it is, and I feel bad about it too."

"I understand that instead of chores you had a cigarette out under the tree."

"Yup."

Eddy turned to the group, "Okay how you gonna bleed?"

The idea was they had not loved Rudy enough that he wanted to do his chores for the benefit of others.

"Eddy, I think we should do a total field day on the yard while Rudy sits in the house and has his coffee. That oughta show him how much we love 'im."

"I think you're headed in the right direction, but it's not enough. Come on, how ya gonna bleed?"

"I think we oughta get up, and without coffee or anything else, walk around the block four times while Rudy sits in here in the warm house and has his coffee."

"That sounds like a good bleed. All in favor? Unanimous! See you all in the front room at 5:30 a.m. tomorrow. No exceptions, except if you can't walk very well. Then you'll wait on the porch for your fellow residents to finish their bleed."

His peers – not the management – made their love

for him known. As a group, they demonstrated their interest in him. They let him know that if he does something stupid again, they'll probably single him out again and sacrifice for him again. Who needs that?

I think the neighbors got used to dozens of men walking in the neighborhood at some early hour of the morning.

When they came back, the whole group continued their routine with a reading from *The 24 Hour Book*, a book of spiritual readings for alcoholics. Then breakfast.

Did Rudy ever not do a chore again? No! He became a very good resident after that.

CHAPTER 21

~

LOVE KEPT IT
LOOKING GOOD

One day everything was proceeding by the plan. The residents were all doing their chores and all was well. The lawn mower was heard chugging along, making our yard look neat and cared for. The wonderful smell of fresh cut grass pervaded the air. Suddenly, it stopped. I looked out the window and the mower operator was squatting by the machine, fiddling with something.

Eddy came along beside me and said, "Okay, let's watch the experts conduct some equipment maintenance."

Soon, the mower operator went to the equipment shed and brought back some tools. He began to work on the engine. Another man came along and squatted and began to talk to the mower operator. The second man pointed to something on the mower and picked up a wrench and removed whatever he was talking about and laid it carefully off the ground.

About that time, another came along and squatted and began to talk to the other two. His focus was on another part to the engine. He took a screwdriver and removed the part he favored, inspecting it very carefully. He was shaking his head as if to imply that his part was in very bad shape.

Soon there were three observers. They weren't actually working on the machine – just giving support and advice. Occasionally one of the observers pointed to something and offered a comment. The three mechanics nodded and continued to dismantle the machine. A tarp was produced so the parts that had been removed wouldn't pick up any dirt.

One of the mechanics filled a large metal bowel with gasoline. All of the loose parts went into the gasoline to clean off any extra grease or oil. It was clear this was going to be a major overhaul. Then the engine had been removed and dismantled. Now the audience had grown by four more residents. All of them pointing and giving advice.

Each part was carefully inspected by one of the mechanics. Somebody produced an old toothbrush for dissolving congealed oil or grease from various parts. Each part was subjected to a good brushing then swirled around in the bowl of gasoline again and placed neatly on the tarp.

It all looked very impressive. There was some vigorous discussion between the mechanics and the observers. Everyone had an experience with repairing a lawn mower and wanted to make sure their piece of expertise was acknowledged. None of the seven or eight men agreed about how to proceed. The mower operator became the final arbiter.

When he put some parts together, a couple of the observers pointed at something and shook their heads. They seemed to be saying that big mistakes were being made.

Eddy and I couldn't hear the discussion, but we could tell there was a lot of difference of opinion.

Soon the engine was beginning to come together. All the parts has been cleaned and inspected. The mechanics assembled it all. One of the observers pointed to the tarp and picked up a small piece of metal. Rolled it around in his fingers. The others each looked at it and shook their head.

"Damned if I know where that thing goes."

The consensus was that nobody knew the origin or the location of that little piece of metal. It was time to try to start it. It was primed and the pull rope was engaged. Didn't start. The choke was engaged. Didn't start. After several unsuccessful attempts to start the engine, the gallery began to fade away.

Soon, only the mower operator was left.

The last we saw of the project was the mower operator giving the mower a vigorous kick and returning it to the equipment shed

That weekend, Eddy and I were at a flea market looking for a mower.

CHAPTER 22

~

HARVEY HOUSE

Enrique was an older member of the Harvey House group, probably in his fifties. He spoke English with a slight accent common to immigrants who have been in our country for a while. He was quiet and reserved until he got to know you, then he became talkative.

Enrique had a very deep spirituality, almost a mysticism. Like many Mexicans, his worldview was almost animistic. This was often a belief system derived from a familiarity with ancient Mexican spiritual practices combined with Catholicism.

Enrique was a little on the heavy side, always smiling and eager to do what needed to be done. He was also very sharp intellectually. He grasped things quickly and acted accordingly.

On visiting days there were always many people showing up to see him – women, girls, boys, and men, often with very flashy cowboy outfits – who all congregated in the house. The living room would be full of people speaking a brand of Spanish one only finds in some rural parts Mexico. The women always brought an offering of food on large disposable trays:

made-from-scratch tamales, enchiladas with an unbelievable sauce, Spanish rice with fresh tomato and onion. Enrique always shared his food with the house. What a treat!

Enrique never dressed like the other men in his family. He wore jeans and polo shirts and tennis shoes. He always had a bit of grey hair hanging down on his forehead. He had had a job working for Fresno County until they fired him for absenteeism caused by his alcoholism.

I loved to talk to him. He recognized the uniqueness of Harvey House. He believed that someone should write about it since it was so different. He fully got the concept of love that Eddy was teaching and practicing.

"Joo know, Rogelio (the Spanish equivalent of my name), someone has to write about Harvey House. Thees experiment should never be forgotten, Hermano."

"Yeah I know. And I don't think anyone else will preserve it in that way, Hermano."

So Enrique, mi Hermano – this is it. I think you are probably long gone at that great meeting in the sky, but I will try to introduce it to others at this late time in my life. Vaya con Dios, mi Hermano. You have hardly ever left my thoughts."

I'm sure Enrique stayed sober the rest of his life, a day at a time.

CHAPTER 23

~

FORT LYON

The staff at the Fresno VA Hospital had obtained access to a counseling school for addictions at the Fort Lyon VA Hospital in Colorado. I was invited by Dr. Epstein to attend and be certified in counseling in their experimental program. It was being sponsored by the VA, the National Institute for Mental Health, and the University of Arizona. It consisted of four months of internship, four months of classroom education at Fort Lyon, and four months of post classroom externship. Upon receiving the Certificate of Completion, one would be awarded 24 units at the University of Arizona.

At that time in my life I was open to most anything. I was sort of going along and moving in whatever direction life pointed me. Being offered the opportunity to enroll in this program and enter a new career seemed just what I needed.

Fort Lyon was an outpost in the midst of the great prairie, near the Kansas border. In the 1800s a cavalry unit left Fort Lyon and launched the famous Sand Creek massacre. That massacre was one of the worst slaughters ever perpetrated against an Indian tribe. Women, children, and old people were all mowed down by the cavalry. It was shockingly brutal.

The Fort Lyon I met was of another world. It had been acquired by the va and turned into the largest psychiatric hospital in the va system. The hospital sat out in the middle of nowhere on an untended piece of land – a dreary bunch of buildings that looked like something out of a Dickens story – brick edifices with huge dingy white columns in front, sitting on grounds that were covered by dead grass and scraggly trees. One of the more uninviting places I had been in my life. As I entered the grounds I felt like I had made a mistake. *Who the hell wants to spend four months in a place like this?*

Fortunately, the program did not provide housing, so we had to acquire a place to stay in Las Animas, the little farm town nearby. That gave us a break from the sad, oppressive atmosphere of the hospital.

The school had established a kind of clubhouse for students that served as a temporary place to stay until we could find our own rentals. I scored a surprisingly spacious apartment in the attic of an old Victorian house. I had a roommate, Alex Sanchez. We shared meals and transportation and slept in separate rooms. There were more students living downstairs. Cozy.

But then it was back to Fort Lyon Hospital and its bleak environment.

Our classrooms were situated in an old adobe building left over from the 1800's the cavalry days. It was neat, clean, and totally separate from the main hospital. Our meals were in the dining hall so if we wanted lunch and breakfast we had to go into the hospital and eat with the patients – an experience still vivid even today, 40 years later.

I was not prepared for what I found inside. It was the heyday of Thorazine as the treatment of choice for severe psychiatric patients. The halls were full of men who shuffled aimlessly along, going God knows where. Faces frozen in expressionless masks. Eyes dead. Unavailable. They would live out the rest of their lives there.

Some of the patients liked to go outside to tend a garden at one end of the building. It was required, when they went outside, to wear a broad brimmed straw hat in the sun. Because of the drug, when their faces were exposed to the sun, their skin could be permanently discolored a florid purple.

I tried to imagine these men in their uniforms – proud, eager to fight for their country. Their pictures on the mantel at Mom's place – handsome, smiling, enthusiastic, bravely going off to the South Pacific, or later to Korea. Then – God knows what –something happened and they eventually ended up at Fort Lyon shuffling up and down the halls in aimless days of mere existence. Wandering around behind the blank emotional fog of phenothiazine hell.

I will not forget one terribly impaired man they had sequestered in the recesses of the hospital. He was devoid of most of his humanity. They escorted him to the dining hall three times a day, wrapped in a sheet to cover his nakedness. There was a kind of savagery in his face. He drooled down the front of his sheet. His eyes were empty, unseeing. They would sit him down and one of the attendants brought his food back to the table. They allowed him to eat with a spoon and his hands. When he was finished they led him back to wherever they kept him, food smeared on his face and sheet, making strange noises.

That guy once wore a uniform. He had been willing to die for his country. For all intents and purposes he did.

I always wondered: "Who was he? What happened? Where are his parents? Do they still have a picture of their handsome young son, erect in his uniform? Do they know where he is now? Do they ever come see him?"

There is no way to put lipstick on that pig!

School was drudgery. Part of it was taken up with group therapy and psychodrama. The four months went by, and I received a GI Bill check about the time I was preparing to come home. Alex had blown out of school so we needed transportation. I found a '66 Oldsmobile 88 sedan with low mileage, solid mechanics, and a dented rear door. Three hundred fifty dollars and it was mine. The radio even worked. Four of us rode back to Fresno, singing songs and telling stories.

As I was driving away from Fort Lyon for the last time, I looked back and thought of all those Thorazine zombies. I felt grateful to be an alcoholic.

"I'm grateful because I'm treatable. Those poor sons-a-bitches aren't. Yahoo! I'm going home!"

We stopped in Prescott, Arizona and slept in an old church building that had no roof. I remember lying there, looking at the bright desert stars and thanking God for my new life.

CHAPTER 24

~

LAS ANIMAS

It was a long drive from Fresno to Fort Lyon Hospital. It took us through Arizona, Flagstaff, Gallup, New Mexico, Santa Fe, Trinidad, Colorado, and a small state highway to La Junta and Las Animas.

Las Animas was a small farming community whose name means souls or spirits. How that wide place in the road had earned the name is a mystery to me. It had a Safeway store, a picturesque courthouse built in the 1800s, and a barely functioning Chevrolet dealership.

One building housed a kind of clubhouse for students at the Counseling School. We stayed there until I found a rental with Alex Sanchez, our driver on the trip from Fresno. We found a nice little apartment in the attic of an old Victorian farmhouse. It had two sleeping rooms and a large kitchen. Nice.

We needed stuff to cook with, basics of all kinds. In La Junta, the closest town of any size, there was a large second hand store with everything, cheap. I even found an old Zenith table model AM/FM radio with a decent sized speaker to listen to music. We had the makings of a home.

It turned out that Alex wasn't much interested in

recovery. He found the local Mexican cantinas far more interesting than meetings, homework, or anything that had to do with why we were there. Alex headed for inevitable disaster.

I settled into a routine. Weekdays were taken up with school and homework. I found an old easy chair and a floor lamp for a corner of the kitchen and that's where I could be found after dinner in the evening.

Las Animas hosted two meetings a week. There were about ten locals who attended the meetings, plus those of us from the school. Some of our fellow students didn't accept recovery in AA. I think it was good for me to see that. I can sometimes get dogmatic about things.

I remember two cowboys who came together to the Wednesday night meeting arriving off the ranch in an old pickup truck. They were the real deal – sun beaten faces, rough hands, and sinewy bodies. They each brought a box lunch prepared for them by the ranch cook. It usually consisted of fried chicken, potato salad, chopped tomatoes, onions, and cheese for their tortillas. It all smelled wonderful!

They were quiet, very polite, but had the look of a couple of guys you wouldn't want to mess with. What really impressed me about them was the fact that they drove about 70 miles round trip just to make that one meeting a week. To stay sober, they were willing to do that every week.

Las Animas

Las Animas didn't offer a lot of nightlife. There was a smelly old bar a couple of doors up from the Safeway. That was it and we weren't tangling with it. We had heard of a place in the town of Rocky Ford (a few miles past La Junta) that had a country-western band. We would gather a couple of cars full of people to go up there on Saturday night and dance. They tolerated us even if we didn't drink. None of us ever slipped back into our addictions at that place.

Once in a while I would get tired of cooking on weekends and I'd eat at the local coffee shop in Las Animas. A small town coffee shop can be the most important meeting place in town. Breakfast was the time it all got done. It was usually full of cowboys and merchants. Any local who came in was greeted by first name and asked to give a rundown on their family, health, and how business was going. Plans were made to go fishing or hunting, or to recruit a little neighborly help for roundup. And the food was good.

When I arrived in Las Animas and being away from Dean, my sponsor, I felt like I was without a tether. I had a lot to learn in the four months at Fort Lyon. Four months in Fresno was intended to prepare me for the next phase of my life before I returned to Fort Lyon to get my certificate.

I became very familiar with the road to Southern Colorado, making a total of six trips.

CHAPTER 25

~

SOBRIETY

Never underestimate the power of an addiction. "All ya gotta do is stop that dammed drinkin' and you'll be just fine." That was my opinion when I first started in recovery. If I could just overcome the tyranny of the addiction, my life was sure to get better. And it was an improvement, no question. But there was still the anger, the dishonesty, sometimes depression, and other issues as well. The anger was boiling just below the surface waiting to explode. It usually gave me a payoff – my anger was intimidating. It put people off. I often won when I got angry.

There was a further payoff. I could make the other person responsible for my anger. "You are making me angry!" It was perfect. I could get my way and you would be responsible for my defect.

Having gone to 13 different schools between the first and twelfth grades, as the new kid in town, I often had to contend with a bully. I hardly ever won any of those encounters. I was not a very big kid. Each new town or school brought dread.

When I reached seventh grade, something happened that changed it all. I was walking down the hall one day minding my own business when an older kid came along and tweaked my ear – for no reason other than he was bigger than me. I was enraged. Blind fury. The bullying of all those years came to the surface. The hair on the back of my neck stood up. Adrenalin surged. I kicked his legs out from under him and he hit the floor with a thud. Total surprise on his face. I jumped on him, pinning his arms with my legs. I punched him in the face then I grabbed his hair and began to slam his head into the floor.

This small town school had grades seven through in one building. Quickly a crowd gathered. One of the seniors, a stocky Irish kid named Frankie Hurley, saw what was going on and he pulled me away. He grabbed the other guy by the front of the shirt and said, "You mess with him, and you answer to me! Understand?" The kid fled. I won. Anger works. Lesson learned.

When I was about 15 years sober, I sank into a depression that lasted for several months. I went about my life trying to keep my chin up, trying to smile when I really felt like crying. I felt I had to put on a good front because I had a big responsibility – I had a staff and a corporate department that served 40,000 employees all over the world. I reported to the Corporate Medical Director. I'm sure he saw my depression, but he said nothing.

The worst part was associating with my fellow

recovering people and being dishonest about my feelings. I would grit my teeth and smile. I felt ungrateful for the gift of sobriety that I had been given. I was supposed to be happy, damn it! If I ever returned to drinking it would have been then. I didn't. I relied on my spirituality, my connection with the universe, talking daily with whatever it is out there.

Get up. Get cleaned up. Brush your teeth, shave, put on a suit, find the right tie. Get on the streetcar, ride downtown, get off at the Embarcadero Station. Go upstairs. Find the lunch truck. Buy a breakfast sandwich. Grit your teeth and smile at the guy who drives the truck. Exchange pleasantries, wish him a good day. Go into the building, grit your teeth, and smile at the guard. He says, "Good Morning, Mr. G." I grit my teeth, smile, nod. I get off on my floor. My secretary isn't in yet. I go into my office and shut the door. Relief. I eat my sandwich. Kathy, my secretary, knocks and hands me some mail. My workday has started. I grit my teeth…

The irony was that I had achieved success. Top of my game. I was honored and respected by colleagues, had a good income, lived well. I was dying inside.

Eventually it slunk away. Quietly, without a sign. I realized one day that it was gone. I wasn't gritting my teeth and smiling anymore. I laughed readily, felt pleasure and lightness. I enjoyed my work, looked forward to meetings and get-togethers with my friends. I savored a good meal and enjoyed the woman in my life.

The depression hasn't returned. Why did it visit me? What made it invade my space? Why did it choose to squeeze the light out of my life?

Was it organic? Was it a genetic gift passed on to me by an unknown ancestor?

I'll never know.

Sobriety is a progressive thing. Just like addiction. The grievous faults that grow during the drinking time are well established. They function very well. After awhile they don't even seem to bother us much. Lying is a big one – outrageous lies, told with a straight face, without remorse. They drive those who love us crazy. Bold lies, obvious lies. They leave the recipient paralyzed in their outrage – sputtering and yelling their response. Until they finally give up and go away.

I could write about numerous incidents to illustrate my hardness, coldness, lack of caring, selfishness, and my self-centered ways. But just take my word for it – I had those characteristics ad nauseam.

One stops drinking and then attempts to live life only to quickly find that all the negative stuff is still there. That which seemed okay before is now unacceptable. The full load of character issues has not gone away with abstinence. It lingers on, but now you are trying to live in society, on their terms, not on yours.

You are no longer the center of the universe. You

can no longer crash through life ignoring the rules of human interaction. Courtesy, honesty, and concern for others are demanded of you. How do you adjust? How do you join the human race?

If you have no conscience this will not be a great concern of yours. We know there are those who have none. I'm speaking to those who have a conscience. You feel the consequences of selfishness, of uncaring ways. Your heart is saddened by hurtful things that you have done. You fret over angry responses to friends. It is you who needs to repair the baggage you have brought with your newfound abstinence.

You got it, Bud! God's first gift to you is abstinence. There are many more waiting, but you have to work for them. The onion must be ready to be peeled.

A word about spirituality: it comes from many sources. I have a friend who played in the NFL. He retired with a cocaine problem. I encouraged him to go to a 12-step program. He didn't like that idea. He didn't go, but he found his recovery in church.

Spirituality seems to be an essential element in extended recovery. When you consider how our life is lived as a drinking alcoholic, it becomes clear that change has to happen. Living the old way while abstaining just isn't going to work.

Let's face it – one of the great gifts of sobriety is bringing about positive change. Recognizing and admitting to past wrongs charts the course. Repairing old relationships frees us from the guilt and remorse we carry. Continuous self-monitoring of our behavior is essential to continuous growth.

The gift of sobriety requires traveling on a path toward peace and happiness. How you find that is up to you. What other disease mandates such elegant treatment?

CHAPTER 26

~

WHAT HAPPENED?

It was like someone had turned on a beacon that shone for a hundred miles around. It summoned the warriors – the ones who had come back from the wars with their lives slipping into darkness. They came. When they arrived, they found a way out of the darkness. Many chose it, though some didn't.

It was a crazy idea – one that depended on the VA Hospital for its life's blood. No veterans, no Harvey House. It wasn't money. It was people that fed the beast. Eddy had devised a way for financial survival – those who had money paid, those who didn't often used county welfare. Determination was our best financial plan.

After a couple of years I left Harvey House and began a new career. Yet, I really didn't go far away until I moved to San Francisco where I functioned in a world far removed from Harvey House: an international corporation. My job was to make sure, if the need arrived, an employee or immediate family member would be offered the opportunity to receive help for their drinking or other personal problems.

After a few years, word reached me that Harvey

What Happened?

House had folded. I was told a new hospital administrator heard of the Harvey House operation and had a meltdown. The conventional versus the unconventional. It was sad, but I had to acknowledge that it was bound to happen one day. Harvey House's dependency was always subject to a whim. Tenuous at best.

And so it was.

EPILOGUE

As I sit here many years later writing, an old man now, what have I learned from this? What part of me is derived from Harvey House? Why do I want you to know about it?

I think I want you to know about it because, in many ways, it was something that never will be repeated. As people drive along that freeway, now completed, they have no idea what took place underneath that ribbon of concrete. The old farmhouse and the other houses are all gone, sacrificed to "progress." The highway makes it much easier to get to Yosemite from Fresno. That's probably what folks are thinking about.

Let's think about those ghosts under the freeway.

First of all, alcoholism is a fatal disease. People die from pathological drinking – and it's a horrible way to die. We are amused by some of the stories like the lawnmower repair, but every one of those guys was late stage. They would have died if they kept drinking. When I had shown up at the hospital emergency room, the doctor told me I had six months to a year. Harvey House was dead serious. All those veterans were on the way out, even Eddy and me.

My sober life has been impacted by that experience. There was the concept of Harvey House Love – the sacrifice of a personal desire for the benefit of another who has done something that might have offended us. Yet, our only response was to "bleed:" "Look at this, this is how much we love you and we want you to witness our love and feel it as you sit there in the warm house and drink your cup of coffee."

"If you are thinking of leaving and going out there to drink yourself to death, you will drag another life with you. There will be another on those cold streets because you lacked enough love to care about him – and yourself, too." Asking an alcoholic to love themselves in the infancy of their sobriety, that was near impossible! But another guy? Ruin the chances for sobriety of another? That would be too hard to bear!

There were the friendships among the men. Danny – the guy with the suit, tie, and attaché case full of heroin – his best friend was a small black guy with a gravelly voice called Little John. Little John was often heard saying to him: "Ah hell man, what you jess said was a total buncha sheeyit!"

Did that cause a change in Danny? You know it did. Those little things were constantly making inroads in the men, subtle but there.

I was at Harvey House for two years. From the first house with six beds to the nearly unmanageable four houses and 80 beds, it taught me that anything is possible. That love and spiritual principles can take you far. That there are men on the streets who would come to recovery if presented with a chance. Especially if they were met with a little tough love, tough but demonstrable.

Those guys could be a *part* of something. Harvey House was a living institution. It had an identity among recovering people all over town.

"Oh, are you one of the guys at Harvey House?"

"Yes."

"How ya doin? Do you like it?"

"Yeah. It's a great bunch of guys."

"Good."

After my certification at Fort Lyon, I applied for a job at the National Council on Alcoholism in the Los Angeles area. I got the job. As I was getting ready to leave Harvey House, Eddy called me into the office and told me that he was laying a bleed on me: "I want you to bring a speaker from L.A. for our Saturday night meeting once a month."

I didn't hesitate. Of course I would bleed. I did it, I think, for two years. Harvey House always left an impression with my Los Angeles friends. We always had dinner before the meeting, the guys from L.A. talking with the residents as they ate. I could tell they were moved. Sometimes there would be amazement, sometimes concern. And many other feelings. Maybe they even got to love.

Epilogue

I slowly got away from Harvey House as my life took its many turns. Two years in L.A., then on to San Francisco. I secured a corporate job in a giant international corporation as the manager of their Employee Assistance Program. It was totally challenging and absorbing. I never forgot Harvey House. Lest my ego get too big, the calls came from Fresno, reminding me of my sober roots. Danny was the most frequent caller. He was good at deflating my ego. I wish I could pull those men off these pages, reconstitute them, and introduce them to you. What a treat!

In one sense, I don't think any of us ever really left Harvey House.

* *

In keeping with Alcoholics Anonymous tradition of anonymity, names have been changed.